TERRIBLE
BLOOMS

TERRIBLE BLOOMS

MELISSA STEIN

WITHDRAWN

COPPER CANYON PRESS

PORT TOWNSEND, WASHINGTON

Cover photograph: Arielynn Cheng

Copper Canyon Press is in residence at Fort Worden State Park in Port Townsend, Washington, under the auspices of Centrum. Centrum is a gathering place for artists and creative thinkers from around the world, students of all ages and backgrounds, and audiences seeking extraordinary cultural enrichment.

LIBRARY OF CONGRESS CATALOGING-IN-PUBLICATION DATA

Names: Stein, Melissa, author.
Title: Terrible blooms / Melissa Stein.
Description: Port Townsend, Washington : Copper Canyon Press, [2018]
Identifiers: LCCN 2017030675 | ISBN 9781556595295 (pbk. : alk. paper)
Classification: LCC PS3619.T475 A6 2018 | DDC 811/.6—dc23
LC record available at https://lccn.loc.gov/2017030675

98765432 FIRST PRINTING

COPPER CANYON PRESS
Post Office Box 271
Port Townsend, Washington 98368
www.coppercanyonpress.org

for my sisters

Contents

[iii]

[iv]

TERRIBLE BLOOMS

[i]

Harder

If you're going to storm,
I said, do it harder.
Pummel nests from limbs
and drown the furred things
in their dens. Swell creek
to flood, unhome the fish.
Everything's gone too cozy.
Winnow, flush. Let's see
what's got the will.
Let's watch what's tender
choke or breathe. Try
to make a mark on me.

Beast

Tadpole with legs.
Hawk with a long tail
that is a snake
dangling from its beak.
The apple limb
grafted to the plum tree,
blue Mustang
with the dull white hood,
Ken with the head of Barbie.
The boy with a new plump fist
of heart or kidney
or some shining pins or discs
or a thick, imperative tube
fastening a mechanism
of breath. What's wrong
with me is you.

blessings

may your harvest fit in a sack
may none of your apples be
sweet may barbed wire tear off
the snouts of your pigs may the
mirror show the scarecrow's
face the moon shine on your
wedding day may the milliner
embroider your bonnet with
nettles the blackberry fell your
dog may your every joy grow a
carbuncle may your eyes go to
milk may the moth make its
nest in your bedclothes the
wind blow sickness in your
ears may your husband leave
you for a crone may his mother
season your cooking from the
grave may corncrakes gnaw
your sour bones a shadow fall
across your shadow the mice
lay their eggs in the mouths of
your children your children
have the blacksmith's eyes may
tracks lead hunters to your door
your fingers melt like candles
may you succumb to god's
terrible kittens may the wolf
carry off the heart of your heart
and the swans swim thrice by
your grief

Birthstone

Facedown in carpet,
arm pinned behind me.
Oh, opal. Oh, tourmaline.
Oh emerald of the cool, cool shade.
A jewel is buried in this
pile I will find it with
my teeth. Pearl from grit
wrought me. Do you know I
have hopscotch and dandelion,
weathervane, watering can.
I have a story, I am skipping
out into whiteblue checkered
yes that is an apron, edged
in rickrack, whipped
by wind into the shape of
my mother. The sun behind her.
Cut out of that light with
pinking shears, steps out
with face and whole hands,
entire: that old apron
wrapped twice around
my waist, kitchen soldier,
jade milk-glass mixing
bowl wire whisk and sifter,
the floured board, the dough's
shagged fist—does it hurt, does it
bruise, would you hand
me a nasturtium,
its orange burnt bitter
carnelian, mouthful
oh where is that jewel

Heir

Tables heaped with meat
and fruit. Plates laden
with roasted juice and what lies
leaking it. He grabs a fist
of serviceberries and purples
his lips. At the last
she lay blue and bloated
as a frog's upturned belly
in the moat. His reign
stoppered in her. All the sapphires
and gilt. All the chalices
ensanguined. He commands
snowbanks of ermine
to line the crypt. Guard hairs
glistering, ensiform. Murmur
of underfur. An avalanche
to keep them warm.

Groundhog day

i.

Fat joy splayed on its belly
eating everything green gives it.
Fur fluffed and cresting
like a crown.
We go around like this,
mowing up whatever we can
and in our own ways, drowning.

ii.

Who am I to say
this leaf is more delectable
or this flower, that spreads like a gown?
Let the groundhogs devour and burrow.
Let green sustain the mouths.
I can't even control
my own starving.

Spine

Cantilevered in blind heat:
this lust in a field
of grasses taller than
a man. He told my body
something it would never
forget and I never
saw him again.
Weak in the knees
is more than just a phrase;
it's a disease
and I still can't stand up straight.

Lung

Flounder's eyes lie
one side of its head.
Tarantula can shatter
falling centimeters.
Sweet jabuticaba swells
from trunk, not limb.
Like snow in June, this white
spot on your lung belongs
to no one, being wrong.

Dead things

i.

This is the season of dead things.
Bat curled up on its back, frog broken open
to the meat, a turtle's pixelated shell.
And all the frantic honeybees.
As a child I daily encountered such death
when the air was close or thundery.
There was the flipping over,
the poking things with sticks.
Look what I found, smeared and bloated.
Look what's living in it.

ii.

Hawk stood along the path
as I jogged past. He eyed me sharply
but didn't stir. His ankles had these surprising
little cuffs. When I looked back
he took off into a blur of coral tail, gray wing.
He shrieks around the property
to frighten small creatures into hiding
and picks them off while they scurry.
In this way his cry pierces doubly.

iii.

She was nearly gone
by the time I went to see her.
A nurse was dampening her lips
with a coral triangle of sponge

and she was rasping, a little louder
when I sat next to her and told her I was there
and loved her though who knows if she knew
though they say they do. Her skin
had grown a size too small. Her eyes
that were ice blue were closed that day;
because I'd missed my plane
I missed their final opening.
She died early the next morning.
I held my mother's hand through this
though we hadn't spoken in a year.
I'm next, she said. I will be, too.

Quarry

As you slept
I was thinking about the quarry,
about light going deeper
into earth, into rock, the hurt
of light hitting layers
that should be hidden,
that should be buried,
and how when it rained
for a long time that absence filled
with suffering, and we swam.

London, Dresden

In the classically laid out fountain koi
slapped and gaped at the surface
like misguided bathtub toys. Like mute
prisoners. Like the abandoned overgrown
goldfish they were. And even more so
when the sky broke upon them,
unleashing flowers of ice. The bodies
took cover as best they could, as bodies do,
within their medium. And the ice kept on falling,
as long as there was ice to fall.

Flower

The ruler left a welted stripe;
the hand and belt, raised letters

I could read. My desk held
parchment, paint, and mucilage,

its lid a face for stenciling—
how ink would fill the ridge compressed

in wood—those cells—compressed
for good—my own, what I was beaten for.

I never learned to play the violin.
I never learned what I was beaten for.

At Easter brushing watercolor on crayon—
what soaked into the egg's white skin

and what resisted—beading there—
It's possible to envy wax.

Sometimes I drew around the mark.
The red would fade, the blue would stay.

Blue shape, blue flower
yellow took. Then everything went in.

Thanksgiving

Swan folding its head
into its wing. That snow—
falling into the water. My friend's
daughter in the car seat,
sleeping. The water is ice.
The plow doing its job
along the night roads.
Night roads doing their job
of being dark, and slippery.
The crisp perfection of an envelope.
The blank perfection of a sheet.
The snow on the windshield
a tunnel of wings
my friend is driving through.
The night, the plow, the street.
His little daughter's head
nodding against the car seat.
His older daughter next to her.
His wife. A family. Over and over
let's grant them safe passage.
At least on this inviolate page.

Lemon and cedar

What is so pure as grief? A wreck
set sail just to be wrecked again.
To lose what's lost—it's all born lost
and we just fetch it for a little while,
a dandelion span, a quarter-note.
Each day an envelope gummed shut
with honey and mud. Foolish
to think you can build a house
from suffering. Even the hinges will be
bitter. There will be no books
in that house, only transfusions.
And all the lemon and cedar
in the world won't rid the walls
of that hospital smell.

Racetrack

Velvet and shit: I summoned it
and come it did. The horses' flanks
are rank with sweat and flies and I
remember you between my legs
achieving for an hour or so.
We parted on the best of terms:
the sweet unsayable loss that's gain
in drag. The day hurt a little
brighter for all that sharpening.
I have a turnstile heart; it opens
madly and shuts just so.
In morning cold, the horses'
breath takes on the shape of terrible
blooms. The hoof-stamps sound less
urgently. I'm not talking about my heart.

[ii]

Anthem

We were all in love
but didn't know it.
We were all in love
continually. Bless
our little hearts,
smoking and drinking
and wrecking things.
Bless our shameless shame.
We were loud, invincible.
We were tough as rails.
We stole street signs
and knocked over bins.
Ripped the boards
off boarded-up stuff.
Slept in towers
filled with pigeon shit
and fluff. We kicked
beer bottles down
cobbled lanes.
Tires and chains.
Chains and wheels
and skin. The world
was always ending
and we the inventors
of everything.

Seven Minutes in Heaven

It's all the rage to sport waxed moustaches
and cure your own sausages
in some mildewy basement that formerly
would have hosted convulsively
awkward parties with spin the bottle and seven
minutes in the dark and terrifying closet
(aka heaven) but now boasts soppressata
strung on repurposed vintage drying racks
and fat clay pots of kombucha and curdling hops.
Personally I've never recovered from the sex-shaped
void left in those closets by all the groping
that should have occurred to me but didn't:
right under my nose kids my age were creeping
into adulthood one clammy, trembling palm
on one breast at a time. There was also
the horror of not being chosen in gym.
It is conceivable that learning intricately
how to butcher an entire hog
and render every morsel might give one
a feeling of mastery one lacked in childhood.
It is the greatest immaturity to believe suffering
entitles you to something someone wiser
and grayer than I once said.
But in those basements and carpools and
playgrounds as I assassinated one by one
clandestinely my torturers
abandoning their foul normal
bodies to compost the astonishing
tedium of the wending suburban lanes,
I was transubstantiating to supernal
fame and beauty and such eerie genius

that entire books were written about my
books. In fact it takes a long time to realize
your suffering is of very little consequence
to anyone but you. And by that time the future
is already happening and you're pickling okra
and starfruit and foraging for morels in urban forests
and suspending artisan mozzarella in little wet nets
and crafting small-batch, nitrite-free data
and maybe even thinking about having
children, which you swore in a million
billion years you would never do.

Wheel

Why do I keep hearing
dryers spinning?
Everything's gone
warm and sweet.
Life's a container
we're tumbled in.
Time the container
life's tumbled in.
Space contains that,
and maybe it's the planets
careening across some galaxy
that make it so hard to breathe.

Peep

Some sit and watch
the lights blink.
Some feed the quarters in.
Some wheedle for
just a little more
for the quarters they've inserted.
They say you get out
only what you put in.
What kind of alchemy is that?
I'd give my whole life
for another minute.

How I

Stupidly. Like a dog,
like drought
flood, like a vole
the hawk lifts screaming
to its first and last
panoramic.
Each want sired
want and I
was drowning in it—
but kept my head
just enough above
the choking to choke
more. A dog, I said,
or rat pressing
lever unto death.
May we all die wanting
and getting it.

Cave

So baroque the way
he looked at me
like meat
like last night's
remains on their spoiled
slab, working
the blade, the blade
doing its work—
it's what I liked
about him, that raw
regard
unmitigated
those walls
carved out of nothing
by firelight
that heap
of bones
on the ground

Semaphore

Barn collapsing in wet clay. Ants
stranded on grass-tips, signaling
like the blind. Sun scraped across winter
in its numb chariot. Fiddlehead, godhead,
the universe crammed in that green spiral—
larch limbs swaying like anemones, tossed—
sweat-streaked stallion hide, unspeakable
grace— the last few beats in a bird-body,
crusted in crimson, muffled in down—
rubber's calligraphy on asphalt
and the bright jewels of machinery, of engine
padded in a ditch of white violet and clover—
She fell where she stood in the grocery line
as all the padlocks sprung open, all the gates.

Vows

He didn't invite me to the wedding.
Am I some kind of ghost? A few roses
blown open. People kept trooping back
and forth in downpour to view
the thorny stalks. I saw the photos.
Am I shameful? Even from far away
you can tell someone's age by how her body
moves. What bird by the steadiness
of its wings. Some trees are simply
more picturesque. Some days
I'm a regret machine. Why
are children always running, is there
so very much to get to? You terrify
the moments. You waste them like this.
And behind walls doors and screens,
everyone you've ever lost
is repeating marriage vows.

Montgomery Inn

Two old people are quickstepping
across freshly lacquered parquet.

It's been years since I've been stuck
at some celebratory banquet

counting calories and facelifts.
At the one I remember best my sister

and her brand-new husband were dancing at arm's length
because she was six months gone

and he a large guy himself. We all wore
dusty pink and my mother sniffled compulsively

into a coordinating handkerchief with joy or shame
or both, I never knew.

My dad had shaved off his moustache
for the first and last time. My uncle

drunk again, an incandescent bulb.
And so was I. I can't remember what I drank—

chardonnay? Vodka concoction? Champagne?—
but I took off early in my Corolla

and swerved home blasting Joy Division
and the Cure. I was twenty-four

and headed soon to graduate school
to get three thousand miles away

and write some poems and learn
to hike the California hills and have

anxiety attacks. I suppose this is where I get back
to the two old folks dancing like young folks

and draw some conclusion or parallel
like how my parents never once touched so tenderly

or if I ended up like this pair I wouldn't mind so much
and that's how I know I'm getting old, too,

since when I was twenty-four and somehow
simultaneously suicidal and invincible

I vowed I'd never wind up old
or writing poems in this flaccid, middle-aged key.

But maybe he slips and drops her on her back
during some particularly fancy dip

and the paramedics are called
and the Sternos are sheeted

and we all go home loving and fearing
ourselves a little more desperately.

Safehouse

Despite lightning, despite god
rearranging his furniture, I feel
safe as houses. When houses
were safe: from mudslides, arson,
quakes. Houses were never safe,
I suppose, from human intent or force
of nature, only the concept
of home, and that's internal, and malleable.
Come to think of it, I don't really feel safe
in this city, in this building, in this body,
what with the tsunamis, and the cancer, and the leaping
from burning buildings, and the fiery
archangels, poised and muttering at the gates.

Crush

When I said I felt like twelve again
I meant a stumbly, ashamed girl
who didn't know where to put her limbs,
whose fantasies were a terrible accident

she couldn't stop reliving. I meant
a girl whom everyone was growing past,
grabbing up handfuls of being grown.
A girl too smart for her own good

who saw too much and felt too everything
and sometimes could barely leave her bed
for all the wounding. When I said
like a kid again, it's the one hiding

in a thicket of books while all the other kids
were climbing rocks and kissing things.
I meant the books I crammed to get away
from them and me and you.

When I said I had a crush on you I meant
a car pinned under itself on the asphalt,
organs exposed for all to gawk, slowing
each unsirened instant to an eon I fell

in desperate, ravaged love
with my own incapacity. Wanting
does not look good on me.

Lion

Split dandelion, peeled down its silvery
stalk, split head eyeing two directions.
In one, I'm headed west in a Volvo
stationwagon held together by a filigree
of rust. In the other, I'm drowning
in the bath, pristine and lavender. Either way
the path rolls up behind me. I could
dazzle in the volts of the car battery.
I could rise, fragrant and redeemed.
A relief to know it's always earlier
someplace else. Somewhere—dear lion,
dear crown, my dear sweet resting place—
the ruin I've made is in one piece.

October

Grace in fury.
Fury in sinew.
How can what's wild
bear such innocence?
I lost a tender thing.

He lay high up
on my chest, one paw
on each shoulder,
head tucked under my chin.
Clung to me.

Not innocence—
guilelessness—
we deceive ourselves.
I never asked
to be anyone's mother.

On the last day
he couldn't use his legs.
The worst thing,
the indelible thing
was his incomprehension.

Portrait of my family as a pack of cigarettes

I'd barter your life
for a brief orange
flame and a lungful

of peace. My whole family
was like that, tobacco-
stained, curling

a little at the edges.
Singed. Whenever
the wind rose, a few

blew away, easy
as an exhale, and we let go
in the way one does

with paper, smoke.
Until the box lay
empty, on its side,

in some dump. Now and then
cold hands would
fumble it, in hope.

Blue ring

The sun is high
you hitch your apron on
the wash flaps on the line
the cotton and the linen

its white is dizzying
these chores I dip the water out
for cows to dip their noses in
the new heads

in the furrows crest
their tender green you dredge
the drowned wren from its ditch
I scoop the hound its feed

the coffee lives on its blue
ring we're steering by its fumes
our blades rust in the shed
a few ache with use

Playhouse

Under a collapse of honeysuckle
and its fury of bees, under a mulberry

canopy, its swaying thatch of green—
that's where you'd find us, when the voices rose,

playing out civility: leaf-napkins, twig-utensils,
acorn-goblets, tea of wild scallion

and mud. Beside the garden's tangled
wire. Chokecherry, thimbleberry. All summerlong

we colluded on a patchwork of dried leaves
stitched together by stems—crimson, bruise, amber,

brick, copper, cinnamon—to blanket us
when those voices called us home.

Quarry

Floating dock and the sun
and a lady with her infant
and a black dog swimming with a branch
and a boy I loved all silken
and mocking me
from his heavy lashes
surprised with bright drops of water.
He was kind but he had this weakness.
We swam together every day
as the water found new patterns
around our bodies. Dog, infant, lady, sun, dock
orbited as they always had.
And nothing would stop growing.

Halt

Before the pelleting and sway.
Before the heads of Queen Anne's lace
are bent down, overweighted,
and the fronds bang out
some frenzied tarantella
and the lanes churn to runnels,
scouring and stranding
unconscionable debris.
For now, the attenuated
hush that is storm's premonition
in leaves before a single drop careens,
that we halt in, every cell attuned
to how soon it will start,
how bad it will get before it closes,
or if it will pass us over.

Vitrine

i.

Father, your antlers are growing again.
I'm between rocks and forest, I've
delayed waking up as long as I can.
I hear only one kind of birdsong.
Mother, your eyes are red as the loon's
who dives down a century on one sharp breath
to dredge up a pilchard in that iron beak.
She built her nest too close to the sea
and it brined her warm white eggs. Failure
is a part of speech. You can conjugate it—
My sister, too, turned deer
and fled. My other sister lifted off
into a fog she deputized *faith*.
We wear everything out eventually,
love or neglect. We wear our very bodies down.

ii.

We each had our own chamber
of the honeycomb. We each had
our own sting. While he was here
my father played guitar. The guitar
was made from pearls. I climbed
a ladder when my mother sang
and hid up on the roof. I grew to love
the thinnest air winter could provide,
its white erasure. My sisters bled
the veins of night, my mom the throat

of day. My family: shadow of a wasp
crisscrossing yours, anaphylactic.
Nectar and venom, one sweet fang.

iii.

The sweet? Well, my father planted a garden
near a wide, protecting oak. And my mother
in the house did magic things with thread
and soap. Kitchen saint: mixing bowl,
wire whisk, and blade. The house itself a landmine
in a field of ravishment—such blossoms as
you'll never see and books you'll never taste.
My sisters plaited hyacinths into each other's hair.
My father trimmed them down each year.
They sprang back out, unruly. Our rooms
were clean; we made a pretty mess. I walked my father's
black umbrella out in lightning storms. I courted
fire in matches, in vapors, in eyes. I called the bolts down.

iv.

Band of locusts bent on a single task:
we ate what grew. I see him on the railroad tracks
walking off toward the low sun. My mother
on a towboat, about to cut the rope.
My sisters? One a doctor painstaking
needles, blood. The other spends her days and nights
widening the moat. I suppose I'm in a meadow
cupping ears to hives, or stepping through
a forest, peeling shadows from trees.
I bring them home and carefully cut them

into another family. This one
speaks in whispers. Its violences
are understood. We held such ordinary
menace in our hands. We crouched and hid
behind each door. We signaled. We froze.
We bolted. We grew new bodies. We rose.

      v.

I once told you of a prisoner I tried to set free.
They found him, white and bloated, miles north
on a beach. She was my sister; I had the care of her
and failed. Food for crabs, food for snails,
food for emery teeth of fish. They loved her well
until the sea refused. My father was a sailor
on the sea of his own mind. My little boat
could never approach; some wind
always spun me round. But how lovely that sea
in a vitrine, and I never stopped trying.
Until I did, when land jolted up solid,
amazed beneath my feet. None of us
ever reached him. How fathomless the trying.

Zero

Papercut contracts the whole world
to its sting. A stubbed toe to its throb.
Oh beautiful contusion, is it wrong
to love your annihilation
of everything but you?
This valley like a thumbprint
in bruised mountains.
This bruising like a flower
of attention. Out in the field,
a starling blurred to an idea
of feather and blood. Ribbonsnake
a mere suggestion. What I'm trying to say
is I have lost the riveting.

Ardor

When we woke up the roses
had all been trampled, blowsy
froth and armored stalks,

and we stood there in
the weighted morning air
wringing our hands. Nevertheless

there was something magnetic
in the slightly wavering complexion
of where they once stood,

in the ground now ornamented
with expensively calibrated
color crushed and shredded.

Oh to borrow for just an hour
in this tediously agnostic
circumambulation such divine

conviction: to move through
this world as a pillar of fire,
an immaculate decimation—

Powder

i. O

Some blade wedged
in. A tongue of meat
and all the marvel of opening
what needs stay clamped
to live. That was me, twitching
on a tine, acid-stung
and gulped for taste
and to a powder
ground what's left:
nacre. Dumbest chalk.

ii. Puff

Vervain, sandalwood, white
mint. Purses, silk-lined,
and a tablet of soap.
Pearl mirror, such spectacle
and opiate. Fur puff
to dip the powder out. Disease
so exquisite it staggers
the days into glorious
mourning: that all the rest
weren't just like this.

iii. Quinsy

Bone-ache, hot. Steeped
muslin. Throat veiled
to pulp, such web, rhubarb

asphyxiate, something
delivered on a spoon
or in a net. All hail
this packet of xanthine,
powdered quease. Stopper
the heart-fist in its own
gone syrup. Quinsy-
sweet, that clot.

Barometric

That weight—
a magnet. Sodden clouds
pressing down everything.
Sphagnum, gypsum, pearl
iterations. Obsidian. Sphalerite.
The woman kneeling on her pain
in the garden, weeding. The woman
sliding into cedar water. The one
collapsed among the ferns
and wild mint. Pentagonal
beetle, carnelian and jade
stuttering in her hair
with all five limbs.

Jigsaw

I asked a soldier about the camouflage
and he said nothing. Kiss that soldier,
place your hand over his heart.
He has been reinserted with missing
pieces and extra pieces. Such
graffiti and noise. Jigsaw
this soldier. Out in the field,
wheat, and in the wheat, weevils.
A helicopter lands in a field
of soldiers wavering like—
These mines dismantle metaphors.
These soldiers have eaten
the flag. Give them engines,
watch their childhoods fall away.

Never said

the fawns had leapt the fence
into the mountain lion's maw
or that the falcon arrowed past,
a vole pierced in its talons,
releasing the most wrenching
cry. I said I cared for you
and had for a long time. Not
that the shoulder of the wolf
was broken when she fell
from the ravine and her pack
began to shy away. That the sundew
had caught the damselfly
in its sticky pearls and it was
lose a leg or die. I simply said
in slanting evening light
I'd like to have a child.

Jealous

in the jaw: wire me
shut so I can bite
back what I said:
our peace collapsed
as peaches rot and sink—
sweet rot, takes hold
a spot then grows it—
that's what I meant,
a piece of meat gone
soft and sweeter: sunk
into what was: our truce
grew frizz like mold,
velvet-blue I nevertheless
ate—intook—accord
so fraught—it tastes—
here, look. The clabbered
skin split. I'll bite,
you'll snarl, we'll part
for good. Let's
leave. The wasps,
they'll pick clean
what we wrought.

Vertical

I spun around
to lose my bearings.
Not a single bird sang.
Not a single word
through leaves
to tell me where I was.
I picked my way
through moss and fern
and mushrooms
of a thousand kinds,
some kicked over
and tenderly white,
those gills. They
hurt. So many things
here pitched and
fallen in. Kindred.
I could plant myself
on a stump and let it.
How deliciously quiet
my feet to mulch
my hands, my throat,
and thought.
Some seed blow past
and root, or root
elsewhere in other rot
feeding all that
aching vertical.

Quarry

A girl is swimming naked
in dark water. She doesn't see herself
as graceful but the water tells otherwise,
the way it loosens and strikes
and burnishes. Exposed
ledges, rock's crumble on surfaces
and the surface of the water broken
by her body, marine and white.
There is also a freckled boy
contained in his body's wish
to outstrip but for now
mere stripling, too slight
for the shoulders and limbs
that pummel and thrash
to make himself bigger.
The girl and boy
pinwheel in the water
and do not touch
but are connected
by invisible currents
their bodies manufacture.
Her eyes are closed
but she knows where he is,
diving from the turtle rock
a little clumsily, the muscles
like lozenges
in his thin legs twitching
as they push off.
Days of this. Weeks.
Then, detaching itself from
sun, water, blasted rock

another body comes,
a grown man, all smiles
and cigarettes
and offering. I still dream
that the red-haired boy held my head
under water
to spare me what the man did.

This house

The storm tore through us
like a child's graphite scraping
at the white page until
there is no white,
no page. Now the earth
is sea. It churns up
all that's buried, all that's free.
There is no holding it.
So we hold each other
and rock, and rock.
I always thought
at the end of everything
there would be something.
But I've already let it go.

Milk

The nurse has made up the bed so crisply.
Tucked the corners' origami
soundly into the aluminum frame.

Your lips glisten, moistened with a square
of sponge. I hold your hand—weightless
thing of parchment and twig—

no more your daughter than a seed
cast from hoof-split rattlegrass, no more than
an asterisk sprung from thistle, caught, wished upon,

let go. I inhale the antiseptic scent of bay,
of balsam. Rooted here, in this cheap plastic chair,
as if I'll miss something,

as if my missing it would matter.
Just as—branch-snap to feeding deer, wing-shadow
to the scuttling mouse—it has always mattered.

The window frames a square of light
white and blameless as milk. I turn from you
and drink, and drink, and drink.

Slap

I want to write my lover a poem
but a very bad one. It'll include
a giant squid and some loose change

and cuff links and two blue ferries chugging
headfirst on the East River at twenty-six knots
and only at the last minute averting

disaster through quick thinking and sure reflexes. Also
a bow and arrow and glossy red apple
I perch in front of my heart. To be honest

my lover doesn't really like poetry,
which I guess is why I plan to write
such a bad one, so he can feel right

and strong and good in his beliefs.
Tonight when I go see my lover
he'll hold me as I've never been held

except by him and then I'll have to give him
back. When you get new things
you treat them like glass for a while

and then get used to them
and manhandle them
like everything else.

I don't want to give him back
but partly it's not up to me
and partly I don't want to be his

old sofa. I want to radiate and gleam
arrestingly until the certain, premature
end. You can compose a whole life

out of these rollercoasters.
You can be everywhere
and nowhere, over and over

life slapping you in the face
till you're newly burnished
flat-out gasping and awake.

Wormhole

In Hazardville
between Enfield and Springfield
near the state line
near the Basketball Hall of Fame
shaped like a giant basketball—
in a hotel room increasingly seamy,
you are fucking the one you want most
and have wanted always
and there's no one to fantasize about
because you're staring your actual fantasy in the face
doing every single thing you've fantasized
and it's like some wormhole opens
or black hole who can keep them straight
or maybe a giant earthquake or volcano
but really more like a cosmic event tearing
open the very fabric of the universe
like in some episode of *Star Trek*
and that's what it's like also to come at the same time
because that never happens either,
your cries interlapping like sine waves
or actual waves of two enormous oceans
folding over one another, capsizing
the space-time continuum
that dictates even if you get what you long for most
some odds-annihilating occasion
you won't enjoy it anyway
because you'll be in your own fucking
head the whole time thinking
how you'd damn well better enjoy it—
but this one time, this one

staggering time, you manage it,
you together are glorious,
and somehow outside that improbable
epicenter you'll leave
a huge cleaning tip for
the world ticks on,
sans apocalypse,
the universe apparently
large enough to contain
even this.

[iv]

Rapture

I once turned to swan
in the post-office line, the people
waning there with their parcels
and address stickers oblivious
to the enormity and genius
of my wings. Imagine a white
white enough, a tender
tender enough to suffuse you
to a child's sleep
right on your weary feet?
But the ledgers and the pencils
and the stamps. The daily adhesive.
The bruise and bruise and bruise.
Take heart, oh beautiful people
of the post-office line. I hereby
lend you my ascension.
In my numb and glorious
profusion I enfold you
and your piglet grief.

Clerestory

By the roots of my hair some god got hold of me.
I survived that voltage and barbed wire.
Now each day is clerestory,
each night a palimpsest of scars.
The militia pulls on its boots and waits.
On the altars, doves peck each other bloody.

A spider traverses its unseen wire
in the rarefied ether of the clerestory.
He told me it wouldn't scar
if I rubbed salt in it. Wait
for the psalm to surface in the blood.
Close behind is the conquering army.

A trapped dove crashes through the clerestory,
a bewildered militia of scars.
I strip the insulation and wait
for ignition: for sweet oil to bloody
the engine. Too late. He's left me
behind, a shipwreck of transept and wire—

you will know me by the scars.
By the crowned and pulsing weight
of every lost and bloodied
thing. Gilded and radiant is the enemy.
His last message traveled the wire
and vanished. God-blind is the clerestory.

All that's left is to hide and wait
for the report of jackboots in a forest of blood.
To some, it is a symphony.

We collect feathers and bind them with wire
and twine. These wings are our clerestory.
The engine stalled, that metal body scarred

the rails, and in its wake, the blood
bearing its testimony.
The bodies dragged. The shallow graves, the fire.
Who stabbed out the windows of the clerestory?
What will annihilate these scars?
The immaculate landmines wait.

We are bound by blood to our enemy
while God feeds stars to his clerestory.
Why aren't they detonated? The whole world waits.

Masochist

We were listening to the song
about the boy who keeps losing
limbs and the girl who loves him
anyway 'cause she's
a masochist. In this way
they're meant to be.
I'm going to talk now
about groundhogs
and how they galumph
across the sunny lawns
of our childhoods. I'm tired
of disfigurement.
Tired of the mirror.
Of the red tail
and the shriek
and the arrows piercing the sides
of the groundhog
and lifting. Even
of the lifting.

Ring

Control was all
I wanted: a handle
on the day, the night
when it curved,
when it swayed,
when I could sense
the teeming stars
in light, in dark
the sun's bare wire.
Some switch
to turn it off:
each shadow
pinned to each tree
like a radius
of infant's
milk it spilled.
And the leaves,
their gossip
of claw and beak
and wind and heat
and wing. Tether
lake to bank and
cloud to peak.
And weather it.
All this to say I've
taken off my ring.

Hive

In the night, fear's stepchild: all hail
the ticking brain. And ash in the fireplace
and in the stove. What am I doing with these
old-woman hands? They don't belong to me.

There was one perfect moment of détente
where you called me the love of your life
but you were stoned and possibly on pills.
Your touch, iambic, when we met
and the rest, sheeted mirrors and grief.

Next door they're perpetually building a house
of schadenfreude and light. They're draping it
in butter-yellow paint. The bees will take up
residence. There's honey in the paint.

Bind

He had no idea
what I constructed for us
in the dark
how my head bent down
or tipped back,
what ugly words I made of it.
There was a tree
a vine wrapped around
until it bowed the tree,
there was a rock
creekwater wore
to slickest organ.
I will carry this lust
a thousand years.
He will bend to it
and stoop to it
and never guess
the magnet.

we have grown nautical

you left a souvenir
on my thigh
it had a mussel's shape
and the cast
of the water's
weedy greens
you made a fool of me
I made you queen
of this underwater
forest I gave you pearls
and lanternfish
you gave me a black eye
you said I'd thank you for
later now
it's later and
the water's dark and still
and still there's so much
teeming
such cold blood
tentacle and fin

Lily of the valley

In the lake bodies shift
with the currents. Waterskaters
traverse their tapestries. On the bank
grow plants that no longer have names.
Some have tongues to catch the feet
of flying things. Two shoes lie
on the bank as well. A child's shoes.
A girl's. Can you see her, dirty dress,
dirty soles? The arms that held her?
In a convulsion of tenderness
that wasn't tenderness. In a fever
that wasn't fever. In this heat
the lily of the valley exudes
such sweetness a man can't think.
All you want to do is stop up
those pealing mouths. Those white
white skirts, unutterably clean.

Lewis and Clark

The air stung with velocity
and need. All the lights veered,
rafters heaved. I starved myself
beyond doors and windows.
I hollowed out seeds
and sowed blank fistfuls
along the wounded furrows.
Balanced the shotgun on broken
days. Made myself alone
enough to frighten me.

Almanac

How many times
can you plough
the same field, the same soil
until all that will grow
are spined and banded things—
a knob, a spike, a bulge, an eye
split from the rind
peering casually
into an approaching thorn—
a century may yield
some gold or pink reprieve
and all the rest is scar.

Husband

Even if you could dredge this river
there's nowhere to put the water.
The land's run out of hiding places—
I've stuffed too many secrets there.
My tumble with the farmhand, rustler,
priest. Arsenic in the pie, sweet
thief. The baby didn't wake. Nor did
the hound, rank snarl of fur. Solely
by my grace do you sit down to morning
rashers, jaundiced eyeballs
on your plate. Husband, they see as I do
the hour your use ends. I have meet help.
The fields near plough themselves, gloved hands
collect the dozens, the milk. I'll soon have
all I need. A truce of soil and rain,
pest and feast. In such bounty
shall my finest secret
flush and swell. In such peace.

driveway

i.

the car   was up on blocks
the driveway fresh and sleek
and fragrant as new
grief   i took
that engine where
it belonged and punished it
a little in the air
that parted for its force—
its guttural tugged my
insides and the day
collapsed and spread—

ii.

i could be dead
and still want you
is what he
what he said

iii.

i'm grease
beneath your knees
i melt and shine
and reek   the car
was up on blocks and i
in it, racked, trussed
like any meat, a cigarette
tucked in the window crease—

don't tell me i'm biographical
i've stained the seats   my eyes are wet
the grass is thick with wings
and blood and i
will not remember you

Grisly variations

i. Mercy

That white disc drills a hole
through another morning.
Something's fallen in the well.
Bald lake spreads itself out like glitter
in dried glue. Two spotted fawns
leap silently, on springs.
Wingless birds command the trees.
All the trees are numbered.
Through meadow iris, insect foam,
pain walks by on stilts.
My scream wakes up
before I do.

ii. Veer

Clean muslin draped over a pie
to keep the flies off. Sour
cherry, say, or lemon rind. A dark spot
on the X-ray. Magpies at the feeder,
foiling the squirrel. Twenty more years
to make a child. A beehive—
all that life stuffed in the walls.
I go down to the lake every morning
to watch the mist rise. Nothing
gets clearer. God a newborn
foal, teetering in the barn. God
in a pilot suit, covering his eyes.

iii. Script

Tarzan swung from limb to limb.
Newspapers told the story
of his capture. It was ugly.
Such kneeling, such caprice,
the net laid out, and silent.
Then a commotion and grief.
Top hats and cigars and flashbulbs.
All the doors and windows
numbered. They taught him to write
in a fine Christian hand
with fine polished fingernails.
I don't know what's come over me.

Eulalia

All day fog sang
its songs of burying.
The world erased itself
and drew itself back in.
A girl once stood
out on the road
and offered herself
to the wind. The wind
a name for anything
that wasn't home. A grin,
a beer, a joint, backseat
exchange. Another state
or state of being. In cutoff
shorts and cutoff shirt
and cut off everything. Midsummer
and the air is tar and sweetest
garbage, ozone,
watered hay. The air itself
is offering. Maybe
she's still waiting.
Maybe long and far away
and blossoming.
Maybe she's in the ground
dismantled to root and bone
and quaking grass and memory.
Each foot of ground
its own gone story.

Quarry

That absence filled with water, and we swam:
kept to the surface, above rusted beams
and weeds and car or body parts, above
sequins of glass, or rutted signs, or cans
crushed to bright coins, or hypodermics.
The water covering that rich debris
was clear and pure and cold and so were we,
diving, careening, all body, all gasps
of bubbled air. Cast off on clefts of rock:
our clothes, and school, and family. Too soon
behind the quarry wall, hauling away
the day's last heat, the sun ducked, mosquitoes
clamored for sweet new blood. Leaving, we'd drag
our feet. But we were lighter for the floating.

Little fugue

i. Vertigo

I captained a ship
its name was confusion
gullsong accompanied it
on the quivering seas
I sowed seeds of evergreen
laurel, wild thyme
they took root in the whitecaps
they took root in the brine
I steered through this forest
I steered by the stars
which were eyes fixed on stalks
of a plant I didn't know

ii. Low

I cast my faith out on the waters
I sank into the brine
all the fishes swam to me
their o-mouths like rings
marrying me
to their kingdom
and then I knew
cure has so many forms
the key is merely
to stay alive

Dear columbine, dear engine

Mere water will force a flower
open. Then with a touch
the beautiful intact collapses
into color filament and powder.
It's all my fault. All hands on deck
to help collect what's spilled.
That could be me beneath
a bridge. Torn up beside the road,
a bloat of skin and fur.
Afloat in bathtub, clean,
blue-lipped, forgiven. Facedown
in the snow. *Why do you*
imagine these terrible things?
asks my mother, or her
ghost. Because the paper's
crisp and white. Because
no slate's unwritten.
Because the ant that scaled
this flower head
has nowhere else to go.

Dead things

Last night the moon
lit up a squashed frog
so gleamily. I saw a bird
I can't even describe. And the bat
squealing in my glove—
dark courier, I set it free
but come morning
there was one out on the balcony
rotting in the blanket of its own fur.
All the dead things hurt too much.
Even the bright things breathing.

What sound

Soon the wet will dry,
hiding emerge. Until then,
this swelling and speaking
of silent things. This is
what a fern sounds like.
Wild mint. The fence and wire
and rock wall and the moss
cushioning it. The ground.
The air itself. The dark.
Everything has a voice
and remarkably the same,
in this pummeling.

Mouth

There was a night in summer
I was a white candle
I made such a mess
in the dark
you made a mess
of me
I ate it up like air
the bugs and earth and grass
my hair a nest
dirt built a home in
you called me dirty girl
I ate that up too
my mouth was full
of mouths
there was
no end to it

Acknowledgments

Many thanks to the editors of the publications in which the following poems first appeared, some in slightly different form:

The American Poetry Review: "Racetrack," "Safehouse"

Beloit Poetry Journal: "Playhouse"

The Cincinnati Review: "Vertical"

Copper Nickel: "Blue ring," "Husband"

Four Way Review: "How I"

Harvard Review: "Milk"

The Literary Review: "Lily of the valley," "Lion," "Zero"

The Los Angeles Review: "Ardor," "Vows"

Mead: The Magazine of Literature & Libations: "Hive"

Memorious: "Lung," "Semaphore"

Narrative: "Beast," "blessings," "Harder," "Heir," "Mouth"

New England Review: "Portrait of my family as a pack of cigarettes"

The Normal School: "Rapture"

Painted Bride Quarterly: "Bind," "Lewis and Clark"

Poem-a-Day: "Anthem," "Dear columbine, dear engine," "Ring"

Poetry Northwest: "Jigsaw"

Redivider (Beacon Street Prize): "Vitrine"

River Styx: "Eulalia"

32 Poems: "Flower," "Never said," "Quarry (As you slept)"

Tin House: "Quarry (A girl is swimming naked)," "Slap," "Wormhole"

Washington Square Review: "Birthstone"

The Yale Review: "Seven Minutes in Heaven"

~

"Anthem" is an ode to Philly in the '80s and '90s. In
"Vows," I owe the phrase *regret machine* to a Matthew
Zapruder poem title. The Montgomery Inn was a restaurant
and event space in Montgomeryville, PA, way back when.
At the beginning of "Wormhole," I play fast and loose with
geography for the sake of verbal simplicity. The first line
of "Clerestory" is from Sylvia Plath's "The Hanging Man."
The opening of the poem "Masochist" refers to Frightened
Rabbit's song "The Modern Leper."

~

I'm extraordinarily grateful to Michael Wiegers and the
entire Copper Canyon crew—you're the poetry family I've
always dreamed of.

For fellowships and awards that supported the writing
of these poems, my immense thanks to the National
Endowment for the Arts, Yaddo, the MacDowell Colony,
the Bread Loaf Writers' Conference, the Djerassi Resident
Artists Program, the Blue Mountain Center, and the
Norton Island Residency Program.

Much appreciation to my Thirteen Ways writing group
comrades for helping me hone these poems, especially Idris
Anderson and Lisa Gluskin Stonestreet. And a special
thanks to my dearest Robert Thomas, whose generosity,
forbearance in the face of my neuroses, and keen insight are
formidable.

Warm thanks to Heather Stein, Carol and Barry Stein, and
Debbi LaPorte as well as to Ron Baron, Arielynn Cheng, RC,
Ed Falco, Rebecca Foust, Ian Goldstein, Marisa Handler,

Erika Meitner, Dean Rader, Kathy Rose, Dominic Santiago, Steve Shochet, Phil Yarnall, and so many others who made this book possible in their own ways.

My gratitude to Mark Doty for setting me on this journey by plucking out *Rough Honey*; Jason Hill for sweet dreams, swimming holes, and research; Lucy Kirchner for design smarts and solidarity in quirkiness; Marie-Elizabeth Mali for support and selfies; Emily McLeod for steady kindness and pho; David Monington for whiskey, beats, smoldering, and extremity; Tomás Q. Morín, poetry buddy and therapist; John Poch for fierceness and feedback; and David Wolfgang-Kimball, gateway drug extraordinaire.

And of course to all the tacos and desert peeps, and the adventure buddies and collaborators who shall remain nameless: may we ever party in the dark.

Melissa Stein is the author of the poetry collection *Rough Honey*, winner of the APR/Honickman First Book Prize. Her work has appeared in *The American Poetry Review*, *Best New Poets*, *Harvard Review*, *New England Review*, *Ploughshares*, *Tin House*, and many other journals and anthologies. She has received fellowships from the Bread Loaf Writers' Conference, the MacDowell Colony, the National Endowment for the Arts, and Yaddo. She is a freelance editor in San Francisco.

Poetry is vital to language and living. Since 1972, Copper Canyon Press has published extraordinary poetry from around the world to engage the imaginations and intellects of readers, writers, booksellers, librarians, teachers, students, and donors.

WE ARE GRATEFUL FOR THE MAJOR SUPPORT PROVIDED BY:

THE PAUL G. ALLEN
FAMILY FOUNDATION

amazon *literary partnership*

the POINT
envision · enact · evolve

4
CULTURE

golden lasso

Lannan

  National Endowment for the Arts
arts.gov
ART WORKS.

A&
OFFICE OF ARTS & CULTURE
SEATTLE

SEATTLE FOUNDATION

WASHINGTON STATE ARTS COMMISSION

TO LEARN MORE ABOUT UNDERWRITING
COPPER CANYON PRESS TITLES,
PLEASE CALL 360-385-4925 EXT. 103

WE ARE GRATEFUL FOR THE MAJOR SUPPORT PROVIDED BY:

Anonymous

Jill Baker and Jeffrey Bishop

Donna and Matt Bellew

John Branch

Diana Broze

Sarah and Tim Cavanaugh

Janet and Les Cox

Mimi Gardner Gates

Linda Gerrard and Walter Parsons

Gull Industries, Inc. on behalf of
    Ruth and William True

The Trust of Warren A. Gummow

Steven Myron Holl

Phil Kovacevich and Eric Wechsler

Lakeside Industries, Inc.
    on behalf of Jeanne Marie Lee

Maureen Lee and Mark Busto

Rhoady Lee and Alan Gartenhaus

Ellie Mathews and Carl Youngmann
    as The North Press

Anne O'Donnell and John Phillips

Petunia Charitable Fund and
    advisor Elizabeth Hebert

Suzie Rapp and Mark Hamilton

Jill and Bill Ruckelshaus

Cynthia Lovelace Sears and
    Frank Buxton

Kim and Jeff Seely

Catherine Eaton Skinner and
    David Skinner

Dan Waggoner

Austin Walters

Barbara and Charles Wright

The dedicated interns and
    faithful volunteers of
    Copper Canyon Press

The Chinese character for poetry is made up of two parts:
"word" and "temple." It also serves as pressmark for
Copper Canyon Press.

The poems are set in Centaur. Display type is CG Alpin Gothic and
DIN Next Pro.
Printed on archival-quality paper using soy-based inks.
Book design and composition by Phil Kovacevich.